A Guide for
STUDENT TUTORS

TITLES IN THE TUTORING SERIES

by Patricia S. Koskinen and Robert M. Wilson

Developing a Successful Tutoring Program (for teachers and school administrators)

Tutoring: A Guide for Success (for adult tutors)

A Guide for Student Tutors

A Guide for
STUDENT TUTORS

Patricia S. Koskinen and Robert M. Wilson

Reading Center, College of Education
University of Maryland at College Park

Teachers College, Columbia University, New York and London 1982

Published by Teachers College Press, 1234 Amsterdam Avenue,
New York, N.Y. 10027

Library of Congress Cataloging in Publication Data

Koskinen, Patricia S., 1942–
    A guide for student tutors.

    (Tutoring series)
    Includes index.
    1.   Peer-group tutoring of students.   I.   Wilson, Robert Mills.
II.   Title.   III.   Series: Koskinen,
Patricia S., 1942–   Tutoring series.
LC41.K673   371.3'94   81-18334
                                      AACR2

ISBN 0-8077-2674-5

Manufactured in the United States of America

87   86   85   84   83   82   1   2   3   4   5   6

Contents

Preface

Welcome to tutoring. You are about to become involved in a very important activity. The student with whom you work will rely upon you for help.

This book is yours to keep. You can write in it, make notes in it, and show it to your friends and family. The book is full of ideas that will make your tutoring a success.

The material is designed to make it easy for you to get started. It provides specific tips and will help you understand the nature of tutoring.

It is likely that while you help another student learn, you will learn as well.

As you use this book to become a skilled tutor, remember that some of the suggestions might not fit your program. Use the ideas that you think will work. Change other ideas to meet the needs of your student. If you have questions, be sure to ask your coordinator.

We hope you have a wonderful tutoring experience.

College Park, Md., 1982   P.S.K.
                                                                           R.M.W.

Acknowledgments

The pleasure of writing these books in the tutoring series was enhanced by the many people who contributed their ideas, suggestions, and enthusiastic support. Special appreciation is extended to the many coordinators of tutoring programs and tutors and their students whose excitement about their work stimulated us to write this book.

We are particularly grateful to John Koskinen who has been a skillful editor as well as a continuous source of encouragement. Marti King's reactions to the initial draft of our first manuscript were also especially helpful. We are indebted to Darryl Henry and Sandra Weiswasser for the warm, loving pictures they took of tutors and their students.

Other friends have also given generously of their time and expertise. Susan Coles and Sharon Villa provided not only expert typing but continuous patience and good cheer. Thomas Higgs contributed a number of creative illustrations for the text. Finally we appreciate the help of Lois Patton, Louise Craft, and Abby Levine, our editors, who have given us excellent advice and guided the final development of these books.

1 Tutoring Programs: What Are They All About?

TUTORING programs have been started in many schools throughout the country. Students are helping one another learn more about reading, math, and other subjects. This section will give you some general information about tutoring. The sections that follow will provide some ideas on how to tutor students.

WHY SHOULD I BE A TUTOR?

There are four reasons why you might want to become a tutor:

- You could help students learn something that they may have missed in school.
- You could help students feel good about themselves as learners.

- You could help a teacher who does not have enough time to give to each student.
- You would have the good feeling that comes from helping others.

WHY DO SOME STUDENTS NEED TUTORING?

There are many reasons why students may need tutoring. A few of these reasons are:

- Some students miss school and need help to catch up.
- Some students miss lessons because of other school activities and need extra instruction.
- Some students work well with their teachers but have difficulty working alone. A tutor can help that type of student.
- Some students don't feel good about themselves as learners. They tend to give up. A tutor can encourage such students when the going gets tough.

If what has been mentioned so far is interesting to you, then read on and we will provide you with some more information.

WHAT ARE THE GENERAL PURPOSES OF TUTORING?

Tutoring programs have four general purposes:

- to reinforce academic skills or activities
- to reinforce physical skills or activities
- to reinforce creative skills or activities
- to help a student feel good about learning

WHO WILL I BE TUTORING?

Generally you will tutor one student at a time. The teacher will identify that person for you. When you know who it will be, write his or her name and grade in the spaces below.

Student's name _____

Grade _____

WHAT WILL I BE DOING DURING THE TUTORING SESSION?

The content of your tutoring lessons will be identified by your student's teacher. That content is usually very specific. For example, you might:

- help a student to learn new words
- help a student complete follow-up work in arithmetic
- help a student complete a short report that was assigned

Content of my tutoring:

_____

_____

_____

WHEN WILL I TUTOR?

Tutoring time will be set according to both your schedule and your student's schedule. It is usually best if a specific time is established for tutoring to take place. In that way both you and your student can plan your other school activities.

Time set for tutoring:

Day(s) _____

Time of day _____

WHERE WILL I TUTOR?

Your tutoring coordinator will assign you a place in which you can work. Make a note of that place here.

Place _____

When you are working with a young child, you may need to pick up your student from the classroom. You should do this until he or she gets to know the days and times of tutoring.

Place to pick up student:

_____

HOW WILL I KNOW WHAT TO DO?

You will receive training from a teacher or tutoring coordinator. The length of the training sessions will depend upon what you will be asked to do. Some programs will have training sessions at specific times during the period of your tutoring. It is often good to hear how other tutors are doing. It is possible to learn a lot from others, and they can learn from you.

Date and time of my initial tutor-training:

Date _____

Time _____

IF I HAVE QUESTIONS OR PROBLEMS, TO WHOM SHOULD I GO?

Most tutoring programs have a coordinator, or contact person, who will be available while tutoring is in progress. If such a person is not there when needed, you can:

- ask the student's teacher
- ask another teacher who is available
- ask another tutor

It is best to have one person identified for you to contact. You should know where that person usually is on the days and times of your tutoring.

My contact person is _____

When I am tutoring, he or she can be found in

_____

A backup contact person should also be identified for you to consult when your contact person is not available.

My backup contact person is _____

When I am tutoring he or she can be found in

_____

WHAT DO I DO WHEN I CAN'T GO TO TUTORING?

Your student will be looking forward to your tutoring sessions and will be disappointed when you can't come. Be sure to let him or her know. You also need to tell your coordinator or teacher.

Name of person to tell or call when I can't go to tutoring

_____

Phone number _____

HOW DO I KNOW IF I AM QUALIFIED TO BE A TUTOR?

All kinds of students can be tutors. Most students do not know when they begin whether they will be successful or not. Use this checklist as a guide. Check those items that fit you.

_____1.   I like to help others feel good about themselves.

_____2.   I am dependable. I can be relied upon to do what I say I will do.

_____3.   I can keep private information about others to myself.

_____4.   I am willing to take time to prepare for my tutoring.

_____5.   I can follow school rules about tutoring well.

If you can honestly check these items, then you have a good chance of being a successful tutor. If you cannot, then you should talk with your tutoring coordinator. Perhaps you can learn to do some of these things, or perhaps you have never had a chance to see how well you can do them.

2 Getting Started

NOW that you are a tutor, you are probably already thinking about how you will be working with your student. One of your biggest jobs is to make your student feel comfortable and happy about working with you. To do this, you will want to learn about general school and tutoring procedures. They will help you get off to a good start.

GENERAL SCHOOL PROCEDURES

As you prepare for your tutoring session, you need to think about general school procedures. Being responsible is part of the tutor's job. You can show you are being responsible by:

- obeying school rules (such as walking quietly in halls)
- helping your student obey the rules
- coming to tutoring regularly
- beginning and ending the sessions on time
- telling your coordinator and student when you will *not* be able to go to tutoring
- not telling others about your student's problems

If you are tutoring in a school that you don't know very well, be sure to find out the guidelines for:

- *Fire emergencies*. Check on safe exit areas.
- *Health emergencies*. If your student is hurt or sick, get help immediately. Tell his or her teacher, the principal, school secretary, nurse, or any other available adult.
- *Trips*. Check with your student's teachers and the tutoring coordinator if you want to take a student out of the building. Written permission from parents is usually needed for trips.

PLANNING YOUR TUTORING SESSIONS

Careful planning is important for good tutoring. Each session should include the following parts:

Helping the Student Feel at Ease.   Let your student know you are glad to see him or her.

- Smile.
- Be friendly.

Working with a Specific Skill Activity.   Your tutoring coordinator will help you plan your skill work. Go over plans before each session and ask yourself these questions:

- Do I understand what I am going to do?
- Do I have the materials I need?

When working with your student, plan to:

- review what you did together at the last session
- make your activities interesting to your student
- help him or her to be successful

Discussing the Student's Reactions to the Activity.   Ask your student how he or she liked doing the activity. The answers will help you plan other activities.

Making Plans for the Next Session.   Look at the work the student has done and decide what you should do next time. Should the work be easier? Should it be harder? Should it be more interesting?

Providing an Extra Activity.   Because it is hard to know how much work to plan for each session, always have an extra activity. Be sure to bring it to each session. You might want to bring:

- something to read. You could use a book with lots of facts, like the *Guinness Book of World Records,* one with simple projects, or an interesting story.
- a magazine or newspaper article on a current topic to discuss.
- jokes or riddles to read to each other.
- word games, such as hangman or a crossword puzzle.

RECORD-KEEPING

Even the best teachers make notes to help them remember what they have taught. Record-keeping will help you be a better tutor. It will allow you to:

- keep track of what you have done
- remember successful ideas to try again
- evaluate the work that has been completed so both you and your student can see how much you've accomplished

Check with your coordinator for ideas for record-keeping. You might want to use a daily lesson plan such as the one a tutor has filled out in figure 1. (The first part of the form was completed before the tutoring session; the rest, afterwards.)

MAKING FRIENDS WITH YOUR STUDENT

Students learn best when they feel comfortable. Help your student relax and enjoy working with you. One way to do this is to discuss his or her interests. Think of questions that will help you get to know the student. Try questions such as:

- Do you like films or TV? What do you like to watch?
- What kinds of sports do you like to play?

FIGURE 1 Tutoring Log

Name _James_   Date _April 5_

Plans

1. Help student feel at ease.
2. Activity _Playing "bingo" game with 20 words._

3. Other activities (planned or unplanned) _Read Frog and Toad Together._

Comments on Tutoring Session (things that happened, successes, problems, ideas for future sessions)

James really liked the game. He knows twelve words real well. He wants to play the "race track" game next time. The frog book is good. We read eight pages.

How do you feel about your tutoring session? ☺

pretty good

- Do you like animals? What kinds?
- What kinds of books or magazines do you like to read?
- What do you want to be when you grow up?
- Do you have any brothers or sisters?
- What do you like to do in your spare time?
- What do you like about school? What don't you like about school?
- What is your favorite musical group?

Pick about four questions to ask at your first meeting. You can ask other questions at later sessions. Write questions you want to ask on the lines below.

_____

_____

_____

_____

_____

Your student will also be interested in you. Be sure to talk about things you like to do.

CHECKLIST FOR THE FIRST DAY OF TUTORING

Before you begin tutoring, see if you have all the information you need. The checklist in figure 2 will help you.

FIGURE 2 Checklist for the First Day of Tutoring

Do you have the following information?   Check the
box when
you have the
information

1. _____   ☐
Student's name

2. _____   ☐
Day and time of tutoring

3. _____   ☐
Place of tutoring

4. _____   ☐
Place to pick up student

5. Plans for tutoring

List of get-acquainted questions   ☐
High interest activity   ☐
An extra activity   ☐

6. _____   _____
School contact person   Telephone

7. General school procedures

Fire emergency_____   ☐

Health emergency_____   ☐

Dress code_____   ☐

Parking_____   ☐

3 Tips for Making Tutoring a Pleasant and Useful Experience

HERE are eight tutoring tips that you may find helpful.

1. Try to focus your attention on your student's strengths.
   - Note successes and tell your student's teachers about them.
   - Tell your student about things he or she does well.

2. Try to use the interests of your student.
    * Ask your student what he or she likes to do.
    * When possible, use those interests, such as football or pets, as a part of your tutoring.
    * Check with your student's teachers. They might know of special interests that you can use.
3. Listen carefully to your student.
    * Look at the student when he or she talks to you.
    * Discuss his or her ideas together.
    * Let the student finish talking before you take over.
4. Help your student complete activities by him or herself.
    * Discuss what needs to be done to complete an activity.
    * Help the student get started.
    * Encourage the student to check all work for spelling, neatness, and accuracy.
5. Help your student to pay attention.
    * Make activities short and interesting.
    * Share your time plan with your student. Tell him or her how long you are going to work on an activity.
    * Help your student know when an activity is completed.
6. Give your student lots of encouragement.
    * When things are going well, think of different ways to say "You're doing a good job," such as:
    "What a great answer!"
    "Excellent! That was a difficult problem."
    "You really remembered a lot!"
    "Good thinking!"
    "I like the way you did that!"
    * You may want to give a hug or a pat on the shoulder as a way of showing support.
    * When things are not going too well, give help by saying:
    "Good, this part is right. Let's look at the other part together."
    "Let's try that again. I'll help you."
    "That was a hard problem. Let's look at that another time."

7. Show that you enjoy working with your student.
   - Smile.
   - Use a pleasant tone of voice.
   - Be friendly.
8. Prepare to read to your student.
   - Set a good model.
   - Practice before your tutoring session.
   - Know all of the words.
   - Read with expression.

These eight tips can be used with almost any type of tutoring. Other ways to help your student will be provided in your tutor-training sessions.

4 Common Problems

TUTORING involves problem-solving. Tutors and teachers always run into problems that need to be solved. Here are some questions tutors frequently ask about common problems they have faced. Some suggestions for dealing with these problem are also given.

1. What do I do if a student does not want to try an activity?
   Suggestions:
   • Tell the student you know that it is difficult, but that you are there to help.
   • Urge the student to try and to recognize that a mistake will not be counted against him or her.
   • Do the first part of the activity together as a team. Then let the student try it alone.
2. What do I do if the student is bored?

Suggestions:
- Reexamine the activity to make certain it is appropriate.
- Let the student make decisions. For example, give three activities and let him or her choose one.
- Check to see if the student might be missing an exciting activity in the classroom. If so, suggest that the two of you return to the classroom to participate.

3. What do I do if the student fails to bring necessary materials to the session?

   Suggestions:
   - Have extra materials available.
   - Check with the student before leaving the pickup area to make sure he or she has all the materials.

4. What do I do if a student breaks school rules?

   Suggestions:
   - Go over school rules to be certain that the student knows them.
   - Try to determine why the student broke the rules. Were there circumstances that would explain the behavior?
   - Seek the advice of the tutoring coordinator.

5. What do I do if a student seems angry or upset?

   Suggestions:
   - Ask your student if he or she is upset about something. You might be able to help.
   - Help your student feel comfortable as soon as he or she gets to tutoring.
   - Develop activities that are fun and will help the student feel successful.
   - Talk with your student's teacher about the way the student is acting.

6. What do I do if a student doesn't understand an activity?

   Suggestions:
   - Break the activity into small parts and let the student work on one part at a time.
   - Explain the activity using easier words and examples related to the student's life.

7.   What do I do if a student gives incorrect answers and I want
     to focus on student strengths?
     Suggestions:
     • Compliment good thinking and urge the student to focus
       on another possible solution.
     • Look for parts of the response that are correct.
     • Provide time for the student to rethink the response with-
       out any reaction from you.

5 Keeping Up Your Interest in Tutoring

YOU are the key to successful tutoring. You need to feel comfortable working with students. You also need to know that your time is being well-spent. As you become involved in tutoring, you should enjoy yourself. The whole idea of helping another person is very rewarding. You can do many things to help keep up your interest in tutoring. Try some of these ideas.

Ask Questions.   If you have a question or concern, talk with your coordinator or teacher. Getting a question answered, even a very small one, may prevent future problems. Some tutors have a sheet of questions called "Questions to Ask the Coordinator." This helps them remember their questions when they meet with the coordinator or teacher.

Evaluate Your Tutoring Sessions.   You will be more interested in tutoring if you feel your student enjoys working with you and is learning. To keep your student interested in his or her work, you have to keep evaluating your sessions. You need to look for things that are going well and things that need to be changed so your student will learn more easily. When thinking about each tutoring session, ask yourself these kinds of questions:

- Was I friendly?   Yes   No
- Did I talk to my student about his or her interests?   Yes   No
- Was I well-prepared?   Yes   No
- Was the student interested in the activities?   Yes   No
- Did I give lots of encouragement when the student was successful?   Yes   No
- Did I begin and end the sessions on time?   Yes   No

You will want to continue doing those things that have a "yes" answer. Try to figure out what you can do to change those areas where you have answered "no." Are there other things you can do to help your student learn more? Write these on the lines below.

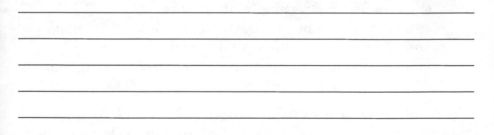

Get More Information About Tutoring.   You can get more information about tutoring by:

- talking with other tutors
- attending meetings for tutors
- talking with teachers and your coordinator

Tutor meetings and informal talks with tutors and teachers will give you new ideas for teaching. They also can help you solve common problems tutors face. Many tutors find it makes them feel good to talk with people who are having similar teaching experiences.

Organize Your Tutoring Materials. Keep your materials for tutoring in a place where you can find them easily. Tutoring is not as enjoyable if you always are looking for your materials. Some tutors use a three-ring binder with pockets to store their daily plans and other information. When you are using things such as games and books for tutoring, keep them together in a sturdy bag.

Look for Signs of Progress. Some tutoring sessions will be excellent and some will be only fair. Even if you always do a good job of planning, your student may be happy some days and tired or even moody on other days. Don't be discouraged if there is an occasional bad day. Try to figure out what went wrong, but also look for all the good things that have been happening.

Look for small signs of progress or success, such as:

- a student beginning to come to tutoring on time
- a student working on an assignment a few minutes longer than he or she was able to do before
- your development of a particularly interesting activity
- your being more patient than usual
- your explaining something particularly well so that the student was able to understand it

These successes are signs of progress. You and your student should feel proud of them. Enjoy finding things that have gone well. They are what makes tutoring worthwhile.

Index

An "F" after a page number indicates that the information is contained in a figure.